SUPER COOL FORCES AND MOTION ACTIVITIES

with MAX AXIOM

by Agnieszka Biskup

Consultant:
Susan K. Blessing, Ph.D.
Professor of Physics

Raintree is an imprint of Capstone Global Library Limited, a company
incorporated in England and Wales having its registered office at 7 Pilgrim
Street, London, EC4V 6LB – Registered company number: 6695582

www.raintree.co.uk
myorders@raintree.co.uk

Editorial Credits
Christopher L. Harbo, editor; Nathan Gassman, art director; Tracy McCabe,
designer; Katy Lavigne, production specialist; Sarah Schuette and Marcy
Morin, project creation

Cover Illustration
Marcelo Baez

Photo Credits
Photographs by Capstone Studio: Karon Dubke

ISBN 978 1 4062 9324 1
18 17 16 15 14
10 9 8 7 6 5 4 3 2 1

British Library Cataloguing in Publication Data
A full catalogue record for this book is available from the British Library.

Every effort has been made to contact copyright holders of material
reproduced in this book. Any omissions will be rectified in subsequent
printings if notice is given to the publisher.

All the Internet addresses (URLs) given in this book were valid at the time
of going to press. However, due to the dynamic nature of the Internet, some
addresses may have changed, or sites may have changed or ceased to exist
since publication. While the author and publisher regret any inconvenience
this may cause readers, no responsibility for any such changes can be
accepted by either the author or the publisher.

Printed and Bound in China.

Contents

JUMPING INTO FORCES AND MOTION... 4

HARD-BOILED DETECTIVE...................... 6

PENNY DEATH DROP 8

MARSHMALLOW CATAPULT 10

BOUNCY BALLS 12

BOTTLE BOAT 14

BALLOON CAR... 16

FRICTION FUN.. 19

PING-PONG WATER BOTTLE TRICK.... 22

ARTIFICIAL GRAVITY IN A GLASS 24

GOING MARBLES 26

GLOSSARY 30

READ MORE.. 31

WEBSITES.. 31

INDEX.. 32

force any action that changes the movement of an object

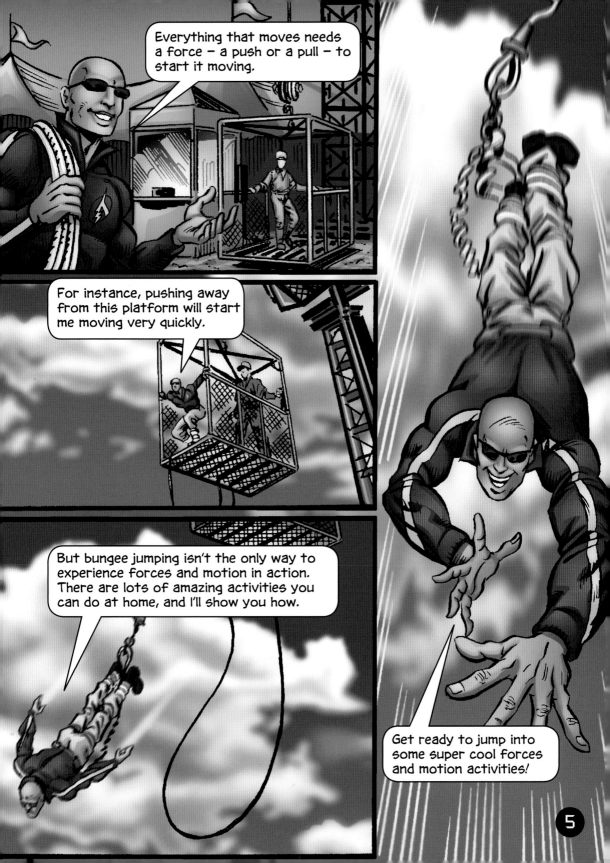

HARD-BOILED DETECTIVE

Almost 400 years ago, scientist Isaac Newton discovered three simple laws of motion. His first law was the law of **inertia**. It says that an object at rest tends to stay at rest, and an object in motion tends to stay in motion. Use Newton's first law to tell the difference between uncooked and hard-boiled eggs. You won't even have to crack their shells.

YOU'LL NEED

3 chilled uncooked eggs

3 chilled hard-boiled eggs

large mixing bowl

1. Carefully put all six eggs in the mixing bowl.

2. Use your hands to gently move the eggs around in the bowl. Be careful not to crack the shells as you mix the eggs.

3. Take the eggs out of the bowl and put them onto a smooth, flat surface.

4. Spin each egg on its side.

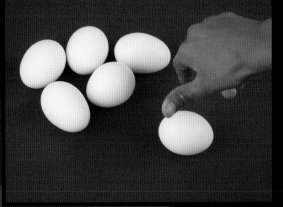

5. Touch each egg lightly to stop it moving and then let go immediately.

6. Observe how each egg behaves.

⚡ AXIOM EXPLANATION

Did you notice that some eggs wobbled after you stopped them? Those were the uncooked eggs demonstrating the law of inertia. When you spun the uncooked egg, the shell began to move. But the liquid inside the shell did not start spinning at the same time as the shell did. When you stopped the uncooked egg, the liquid didn't stop moving straight away either. Its movement inside the shell made the egg wobble. A hard-boiled egg's solid centre, on the other hand, spun and stopped at the same time as its shell.

inertia object's tendency to stay at rest or keep moving at the same speed and in the same direction until a force acts on the object

PENNY DEATH DROP

A resting object's tendency to stay at rest doesn't sound very exciting. But this super cool coin trick will amaze your friends using the power of inertia.

YOU'LL NEED

cardboard or
other stiff paper

ruler

scissors

tape

small jar

water

penny

wooden skewer

1. Measure and cut a 2-centimetre wide by 24-cm long strip from the piece of cardboard.

2. Make the strip into a ring and tape the ends together.

3. Fill the jar with water.

4. Place the ring vertically on top of the jar.

6. Put the skewer through the middle of the ring and very quickly flick the ring off to the side.

5. Balance the penny on top of the ring, over the middle of the jar.

7. Watch where the coin goes.

AXIOM EXPLANATION

If you flicked the ring quickly enough the coin would have landed in the water with a splash. But why didn't the coin follow the ring across the room? Because the coin has inertia. It's at rest while it sits on top of the ring. When you flick the ring, the skewer's forward motion is transferred to the ring, not the coin. The force of gravity pulls the coin down into the jar.

gravity   force that pulls objects with mass together; gravity is what pulls objects down towards the centre of Earth

MARSHMALLOW CATAPULT

You may not break into any fortresses with this marshmallow catapult, but you will see amazing forces in action. Better still, you'll be able to eat your siege machine when you've finished with it!

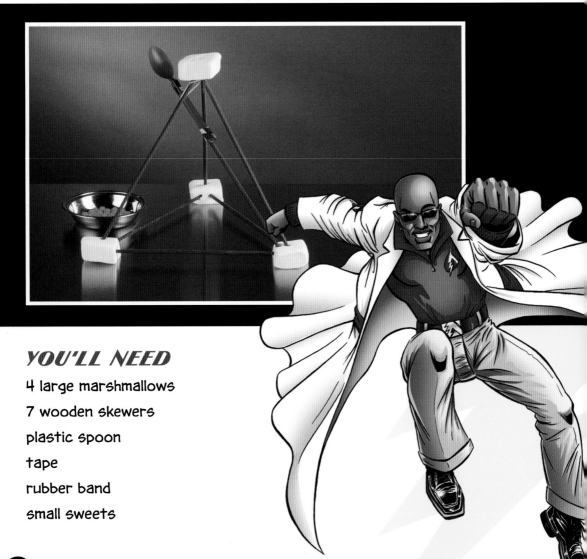

YOU'LL NEED

4 large marshmallows

7 wooden skewers

plastic spoon

tape

rubber band

small sweets

PLAN OF ACTION

1. Connect three marshmallows with three skewers to make a triangle. Lay the triangle on a flat surface.

2. Insert one skewer vertically into each marshmallow in the triangle. Angle these three skewers to form a pyramid. Stick the last marshmallow on the point of the pyramid to keep the structure together.

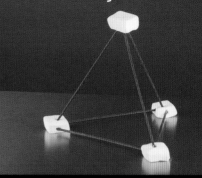

3. Tape the spoon to the end of the remaining skewer.

4. Put the rubber band around the top point of the pyramid.

5. Insert the skewer with the spoon through the rubber band and into one of the marshmallows at the base of the pyramid.

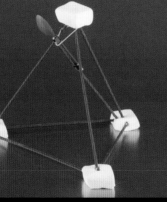

6. Let the catapult sit for at least 24 hours so the marshmallows can harden.

7. Place a small sweet on the spoon. Gently pull the spoon back and release it to fire the catapult.

⚡ AXIOM EXPLANATION

Newton's second law of motion says that when a force acts on an object, the object's movement will change. The more mass an object has, the more force it takes to move it. When you pull the catapult's "arm" back and release it, you apply a force to the sweet. That force accelerates the sweet across the room. Newton's second law also says that the greater the force on an object, the greater the change in movement. Pull the catapult's arm back more and less to see Newton's law in action.

mass amount of material in an object

accelerate change the speed and/or direction of a moving object

BOUNCY BALLS

A tennis ball bounces well on its own. But try teaming it with a basketball. You'll see how **momentum** turns an ordinary bounce into a super one!

YOU'LL NEED

tennis ball

basketball

PLAN OF ACTION

1. Find an open area of hard surface, such as an empty car park or an empty driveway.

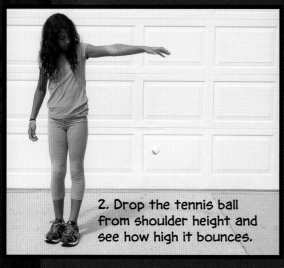

2. Drop the tennis ball from shoulder height and see how high it bounces.

3. Drop the basketball from shoulder height and see how high it bounces.

4. Put the tennis ball on top of the basketball, and drop them together from shoulder height again. What happens to the tennis ball?

AXIOM EXPLANATION

Momentum is the measure of an object's motion. It is equal to the object's mass times its velocity. The basketball has more momentum as it falls because it has more mass than the tennis ball. When the basketball hits the ground, some of that momentum passes into the ground. But the remaining momentum passes to the tennis ball. The tennis ball has less mass than the basketball, which means it will gain a greater velocity. This additional momentum sends the tennis ball soaring.

momentum amount of motion an object carries

velocity speed and direction of a moving object

BOTTLE BOAT

Some boats are powered by the wind, others by petrol. To see Newton's third law of motion in action, you'll power a boat using bicarbonate soda and vinegar!

YOU'LL NEED

plastic drinks bottle with cap

small scrap of wood

small nail

hammer

15 mL bicarbonate soda

5 marbles

125 mL vinegar

large tray of water or bath

PLAN OF ACTION

1. Place the bottle's cap on the scrap of wood. Ask an adult to help you punch a hole in the cap by hammering the nail through it.

2. Put the bicarbonate soda inside the bottle.

3. Add marbles to the bottle to weigh it down.

4. Pour in the vinegar and quickly put the cap back onto the bottle.

5. Tip the bottle so the marbles roll near the cap. Then place the bottle into the tray so the cap is under water.

⚡ AXIOM EXPLANATION

Newton's third law states that for every action, there is an opposite and equal reaction. By actions, Newton meant forces. When vinegar and bicarbonate soda mix together, they react and produce carbon dioxide gas. The gas wants to escape through the hole in the cap. The escaping gas pushes against the water and moves the boat forwards. The action is the gas rushing out of the hole. The reaction is the boat moving forwards.

BALLOON CAR

Rockets use the force of **thrust** to launch into outer space. You'll use the force of thrust to launch a balloon car across the room.

YOU'LL NEED

small balloon

flexible plastic straw

flat wooden craft stick

2 straight plastic straws

4 round hard sweets with holes in the middle

tape

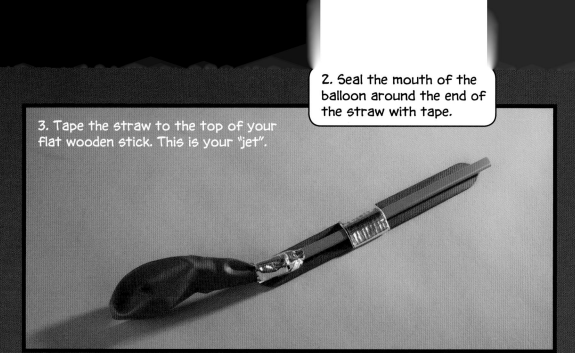

2. Seal the mouth of the balloon around the end of the straw with tape.

3. Tape the straw to the top of your flat wooden stick. This is your "jet".

4. Slip two sweets onto a straight straw. Bend back and tape the tips of the straw on both ends so that the sweets can't fall off. Repeat with the second straight straw.

thrust force that pushes an object in a given direction

continued

5. Tape the straws with the sweets to the bottom of your flat stick. One should be directly below the balloon. These are your "wheels." Make sure they can spin freely.

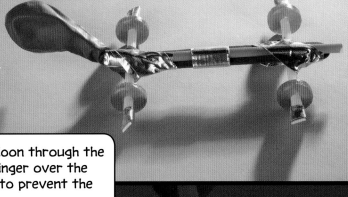

6. Blow up the balloon through the straw. Put your finger over the end of the straw to prevent the air escaping.

7. Place your car on a smooth surface. Adjust the flexible straw so the balloon doesn't touch the surface.

8. Release your finger from the straw and let the car go.

⚡ AXIOM EXPLANATION

Newton's third law of motion is at work once again. The balloon's stored air creates thrust that moves the car forwards. When the air in the balloon moves in one direction, it pushes the car in the opposite direction. This is the same way that rockets work. A rocket pushes gas out of its engines. Then the gas pushes back on the rocket and lifts it into space.

FRICTION FUN

Why do people and cars slip and slide on ice? The key is **friction** – or the lack of it! See how things move differently when friction is reduced.

YOU'LL NEED

cardboard shoebox
without lid

scissors

balloon

masking tape

tape measure

notebook

pencil

box of plastic
drinking straws

friction force created when two objects rub together; friction slows objects down

continued

PLAN OF ACTION

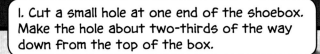

1. Cut a small hole at one end of the shoebox. Make the hole about two-thirds of the way down from the top of the box.

2. Insert the balloon's neck through the hole from the inside of the box.

3. Mark a starting position on the floor with a piece of masking tape.

4. Blow up the balloon and hold it closed with your fingertips.

5. While still holding the balloon closed, place the box on the floor at the starting position. The end of the shoebox opposite the end with the hole in it should align with the tape.

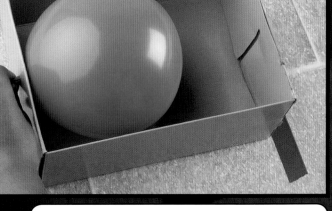

6. Let go of the balloon and measure how far the box has travelled from the starting point. Write it down in your notebook.

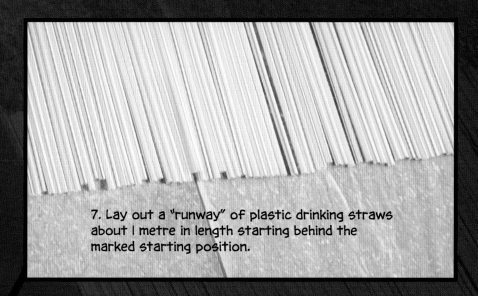

7. Lay out a "runway" of plastic drinking straws about 1 metre in length starting behind the marked starting position.

8. Inflate the balloon in the box, and holding the balloon closed, put the box on top of your runway.

9. Release the balloon. Measure how far the box travels. Write down your result and compare it to the first.

⚡ AXIOM EXPLANATION

Whenever two objects rub against each other, they cause friction. Friction is a force that works against motion. There are different types of friction. On a flat surface, the box is working against sliding friction. But on the straw runway, the box is working against rolling friction. Rolling friction occurs when a round surface rolls over another surface. Your box overcomes rolling friction more easily than sliding friction, so it should have moved further along the straw runway.

PING-PONG WATER BOTTLE TRICK

Can you feel the pressure? You don't notice it, but the air around you constantly pushes on your body. Check out the surprising power of **air pressure** with a ping-pong ball and a bottle of water.

YOU'LL NEED

empty glass bottle

jug of water

plastic dish

ping-pong ball

PLAN OF ACTION

1. Put the glass bottle in the middle of the large plastic dish.

2. Fill the bottle with water until it overflows.

3. Put the ping-pong ball on the mouth of the bottle. A little bit of the water should come out.

4. Pick the bottle up and carefully turn it upside down over the dish.

⚡ AXIOM EXPLANATION

If the force of gravity pulls on the water and the ping-pong ball, why don't they both fall away from the bottle when you turn it upside down? The answer lies in the shape of the ball. It is a sphere with a lot of surface area. The air pressure all around the sphere stops the ball falling out. Ordinary air pressure is 1 kilogram per square centimetre. It provides enough force to keep the ball sealed to the bottle.

air pressure weight of air pushing against something; because air is a fluid, the pressure forces push equally in all directions

ARTIFICIAL GRAVITY IN A GLASS

Some theme parks have a ride called the Gravitron. Riders stand against the inner wall of a giant spinning cylinder while the floor drops out. The spinning motion keeps the riders pinned to the wall without them slipping down. You can create your own mini artificial-gravity ride using a glass and a marble.

YOU'LL NEED

smooth-sided drinking glass

marble

PLAN OF ACTION

1. Hold the glass upright by gripping its flat base with one hand.

2. Put the marble in the bottom of the glass.

4. While still swirling the glass, tilt it on its side. The marble should continue spinning in a circle.

3. Start swirling the glass so that the marble moves in a circle.

5. Turn the glass upside down as you continue swirling.

⚡ AXIOM EXPLANATION

On a very tiny scale, you've just created artificial gravity! The force that keeps the marble moving in a circle is called centripetal force. Any object in motion tends to stay in motion in a straight line, unless something gets in its way. In this case, the curved shape of the glass makes the marble change direction. At the same time, the friction between the marble and the glass prevents the marble from falling out.

centripetal force force that pulls an object turning in a circle inwards towards the centre

GOING MARBLES

Centripetal force keeps you in your seat when you go upside down on a roller coaster. It gives you a push when you're inside a car that's turning quickly. It even stops satellites falling out of the sky. But to see actual evidence of this invisible force, all you need is a marble and some jelly.

YOU'LL NEED

2 clear plastic cups

hole punch

duct tape

46 cm string

saucepan

measuring jug

1 packet of cherry jelly

1 packet of lemon jelly

marble

torch

SAFETY FIRST

Ask an adult to help you make the jelly because you will need to use boiling water.

PLAN OF ACTION

1. Make a hole about 2.5 cm from the top rim of a plastic cup with the hole punch. Make a second hole directly opposite the first hole.

2. Stick small pieces of duct tape over the edge of the cup above each hole. The tape should extend to, but not cover, the holes.

3. Thread the string through the holes and tie the ends securely to the edge of the cup.

4. Follow the directions on the packet to make the lemon jelly.

5. Half fill the unused plastic cup with the lemon jelly.

continued

6. Put the cup in the fridge for about four hours to give the jelly time to set.

7. Remove the cup from the fridge and gently press a marble into the jelly. Allow half of the marble to remain above the jelly's surface.

8. Follow the directions on the packet to make the cherry jelly. Carefully pour this mixture on top of the lemon jelly. Leave about 2.5 cm of space at the top of the cup.

9. Place the cup back in the fridge for another four hours, until the cherry jelly has completely set.

10. Remove the cup from the fridge and stack it inside the cup with the string attached.

11. Find an open area outside. Hold the string handle and swing the stacked cups quickly for 20 complete revolutions next to your body. Make sure you turn in a complete circle every time.

...emove the inner cup and ...a torch through the jelly ...ure to see if the marble ...moved.

...XIOM EXPLANATION

...he marble should have moved to the bottom of the cup. While the ...nts of the cup "want" to move in a straight line, the cup pushes ...inwards. The tension in the string provides the centripetal force on ...p, and the cup provides the centripetal force on the jelly. Because ...lly isn't completely solid, the marble moves through it until it ...es the bottom of the cup. This is the same force that keeps you ...in your seat when you're upside down in a loop on a roller coaster.

Glossary

accelerate change the speed and/or direction of a moving object

air pressure weight of air pushing against something; because air is a fluid, the pressure forces push equally in all directions

centripetal force force that pulls an object turning in a circle inwards towards the centre

force any action that changes the movement of an object

friction force created when two objects rub together; friction slows down objects

gravity force that pulls objects with mass together; gravity is what pulls objects down towards the centre of Earth

inertia object's tendency to stay at rest or keep moving at the same speed and in the same direction until a force acts on the object

mass amount of material in an object

momentum amount of motion an object carries

thrust force that pushes an object in a given direction

velocity speed and direction of a moving object

Read More

Forces and Motion (Essential Physical Science),
Angela Royston (Raintree, 2013)

Forces and Motion: Investigating a Car Crash (Anatomy of an
Investigation), Ian Graham (Raintree, 2014)

Isaac Newton (Science Biographies), Kay Barnham
(Raintree, 2014)

Websites

**www.bbc.co.uk/schools/scienceclips/ages/10_11/forces_
action_fs.shtml**
Discover how different gradients and objects impact upon
the distance a truck can travel when playing this forces in
action game.

www.sciencemuseum.org.uk/launchpad/launchball/
Explore the London Science Museum's games page and play
the Launchball game. Use different sources of force and
motion to slide, bounce and spring your ball into its goal.

Index

acceleration 11
action and reaction 15
air pressure 22–23
artificial gravity 24–25

balloon cars 16–18
balls 12–13, 22–23
bicarbonate soda 14–15
boats 14–15

carbon dioxide 15
catapults 10–11
centripetal force 25, 26–29
chemical reactions 15

eggs 6–7

friction 19–21

gravity 9, 23, 24, 25

inertia 6–7, 8–9

marbles 14–15, 24–25, 26–29
mass 11, 13
momentum 12–13

Newton, Isaac 6
    first law of motion 6
    second law of motion 11
    third law of motion 14–15, 18

pulling forces 5
pushing forces 5

rockets 16, 18

satellites 26
spheres 23

theme park rides 24, 26, 29
thrust 16–18
tricks 8–9, 22–23

velocity 13
vinegar 14–15